# Eleme

## Writing

by Jean Janzen

*Jean Janzen* (signature)

*For Jack,
who practices faithful
writing. Thank you for the
invitation to Houghton —
Jean
April 17, 2007*

Bethel College
North Newton, Kansas
2004

Co-published with
Pandora Press
Kitchener, Ontario

We thank Good Books, Intercourse, Pennsylvania, for permission to reprint portions of the following previously published works: "Glocken" from *Snake in the Parsonage* (1995); "At Summer's End," "Lakes," "The Language of Light," "The Mountain," "Reading the Fields," "Window Facing East," "Window Facing North," "Window Facing South," and "Window Facing West" from *Tasting the Dust* (2000); "Broken Places," "Egrets," "In January," "Night Falls on the Neighborhood," "Piano in the Vineyard," "Seeking the Song," "Wailing in the Shower," and "Wilderness" from *Piano in the Vineyard* (2004).

Library of Congress Cataloging-in-Publication Data

Janzen, Jean.
    Elements of faithful writing / by Jean Janzen.
        p. cm. – (Cornelius H. Wedel historical series ; 13)
    Includes bibliographical references.
    ISBN 1-889239-03-8 (pbk.)
    1. Religion and poetry. 2. Christian poetry–History and criticism. I. Title. II. Series.

PN1077.J26 2004
809.1'93823–dc22

2004055403

Cover illustration by Peter Janzen, "Canal Walk," oil, 18x24, 2002.

Wedel Series logo by Angela Goering Miller

ISBN 1-889239-03-8

Copies available at www.pandorapress.com

# Cornelius H. Wedel Historical Series

Series editor: vols. 1-4, David A. Haury
              vols. 5-13, John D. Thiesen

# Contents

# Series Preface

The Cornelius H. Wedel Historical Series was initiated by the Mennonite Library and Archives at Bethel College as part of the college centennial celebration in 1987. Cornelius H. Wedel, the first president of Bethel College from the beginning of classes in 1893 until his death in 1910, was an early scholar of Mennonite studies. His four volume survey of Mennonite history, published from 1900 to 1904, helped to rescue Anabaptism and Mennonitism from their marginal and denigrated portrayal in standard works of church history. Wedel saw Anabaptism and Mennonitism as part of a tradition of biblical faithfulness going back to the early church.

Wedel also believed in the cultivation of the intellect in all fields of knowledge. The current college mission statement continues the commitment to intellectual, cultural, and spiritual leadership for the church and society. The Wedel Series furthers these goals by publishing research in Mennonite studies with a special emphasis on works with a connection to Bethel College, such as campus lecture series and projects based on the holdings of the Mennonite Library and Archives.

Of the twelve volumes published in the series prior to this time, ten have originated in campus lecture series or symposia, four arose out of library or archival holdings at Bethel College, and two had both ties. One volume has been reprinted since its original publication. Topics in the series have included Mennonite identity, biography and autobiography, Bethel College history, nonviolent interpretations of United States history, Menno Simons, Mennonite literature, and theology.

The volume you have before you continues the dialogue in the series on Mennonite literature in the rich words of distinguished poet Jean Janzen.

John D. Thiesen
Series Editor

# Introduction

I wish to sincerely thank the Menno Simons Lecture Committee for inviting me to be the lecturer for the 2003 series. I feel deeply honored, and hope that my words will offer nourishment to you, the listeners, and now, readers.

Coming to Kansas for these lectures carried weight for me. This is the state where I made the most significant choices of my life. I received catechism from my own father here at Inman where he pastored a house church while a student finishing his degree at Tabor College. Then I was baptized by my brother, Orlando Wiebe, in Meade where he was pastor at the time. I chose to say "yes" to Louis Janzen when he proposed to me in California Hall when I was a Tabor student. He was giving me my engagement ring, slipping it on my finger as we sat in a car overlooking Marion Lake, and just then a park ranger shone his flashlight into the car window and asked, "Are you catching any fish?" A year later we were married in Meade, where my father then was pastor. These "sacramental choices," one might call them, are all connected with the senses, the memory of place, of sun and wind, moon and stillness, dust and mud, and water. And all these choices are associated with language—vows, statements of confession, love letters, hymns, songs, stories and jokes. And the Scriptures.

The other weight I carried into these lectures is the excellence of the series. I was the fifty-second lecturer attempting to honor the life of Menno Simons. And I was the third one to say something about Mennonites and literature, or writing. The lectures of John Ruth in 1976 and Al Reimer in 1991 have been important sources in my own development. Ruth's eloquent call to write out of the center of our communities and their stories was a major source of encouragement when I began writing poems in 1980.[1] Al Reimer's evaluation of the growing community of writers with their various relationships to our Mennonite story continues to illuminate my appreciation and understanding.[2]

---

[1] John L. Ruth, *Mennonite Identity and Literary Art* (Scottdale, Pa.: Herald Press, 1978).

[2] Al Reimer, *Mennonite Literary Voices: Past and Present* (North Newton, Kans.: Bethel College, 1993).

I chose the overall title *Elements of Faithful Writing*, based on the four elements. The faithful artist and writer calls us not only to remember, but also to reclaim our connections with the original, primal materials of our existence. And so I invite you to meditate with me on elemental things. I have grouped my comments based on the periodic table of elements of the ancients—Earth, Air, Water, and Fire. These people believed that all things were made of these four energies, and that each carried physical and symbolic richness.

Four elements, four chapters. However, as you see, I have tweaked them a bit in my naming them mud, water, and fire and air grouped together. The final topic, "Text: Marking the Stone," circles back to earth and recognizes the interconnectedness of the four.

I chose the four elements because our life experiences cannot be recorded in abstract language. Our senses and our words are ever connected to the elements, the concrete representations of our existence. These four are true to my own story of writing, as well as the writers of literature throughout the past millennia. I also chose them as associated with the story of Menno Simons. Having had the privilege of travel in Holland several times, absorbing places and stories in one month-long stay in 1996, I could have chosen the title, "Reading the Fields," which is a poem inspired by Menno Simons' important work with words. The poem was also inspired by the etching by Jan Gleysteen of a Dutch landscape of fields, a narrow lane bordered by tall trees, and in the distance a small house with lighted windows, the suggestion of Menno writing at night. The epigraph for this poem are his words about how the Gospel is preached: ". . . through mouth and pen, with possessions and blood, with life and death."

I begin the poem with these lines: "The tulips unfold their pages,/ field after field in brilliant illuminations." They are "like a story/ of happily-ever-after." It is "a brief singing," for soon they are harvested and the field is bare. Nothing remains except the bulbs hidden in the ground which become "each one a lit window" with "someone leaning into the next word."[3]

---

[3]Jean Janzen, *Tasting the Dust* (Intercourse, PA: Good Books, 2000), 42.

My own "brief singing" is offered in appreciation for the words written down by Menno Simons, so vital to the establishment of our heritage of faith, and with the prayer and hope that someone will be "leaning into the next word." Closely associated with this exploration is my poem, "Reclaiming the Land."

1

Not even Kansas is as flat as this place,
our eyes interrupted only by the distant
dikes where a sailboat is a speck
floating above the land. Land and sea,
elemental, separated as in God's third day.
Order out of chaos. And great emptiness.

Twelfth Century, Hadewijch the Mystic gathers
the young sisters around her, pleads
with them to cherish their emptiness,
to be tender toward their human longings.
They stand in a huddle in the marshy field.
The tree is upside-down, she says, eyes
searching, hats and skirts flapping.
Inside, that burning.

2

These are my people near the breaking
rage of the North Sea, and inland
by the quiet avenues of water—

Menno Simons' escape routes
and his arteries of faith. What footings
here for the descendants,

what moorings for the heavy cargo
of ourselves? The light stays long
in the Dutch summer. Green promises

more green even as I sleep. This land,
reclaimed, opens and fills—country manors,
barns, ships that sailed away and returned

heavy-laden, captains that demanded
blood, and these people with my name
refusing, cutting the ropes, letting it go.

3

"Mennoniten? Sie spielen nicht,
sie trinken nicht, sie lachen nicht,"
say our friends from across the Ems.
Separation from the world? The words
shift like global waters, mirror
the fickle sky.

The land lies uneasily
beside the ocean's strength.
Winds strain at the locked gears
of windmills. One sweeps and dries
the damp fields, another
carries floods in its arms.
Which wind? Which true one
for the turning?

4

In his "View of Haarlem"
Ruisdael's sky dominates
the land. Great thunderheads
rise over the far dikes, faces
of beauty and danger over
the fields of grain, the red
slanted roofs, the dark clusters
of elms and chestnuts.
What we want is hidden,
something elemental that stirs
in the color or in the canvas
itself. Something under
those long stretches of white
linen drying in that shaft
of sunlight.[4]

Only after I had chosen the theme for these lectures did I
realize how appropriate this poem would be as a beginning
interrogation of the elements. They are all here, and they call to
me as a Mennonite Christian who is human. Here is the
landscape of my heritage inviting me to remember the primal
materials of our lives. Here is the mystery of its meaning—the
upside-down tree, the water as threat and as gift, the wind as
power and danger. Here are the questions of separation and of
integration, the unpredictable sky, the longing for beauty. And
here is the primary quest for what lies hidden, and what can
save us.

---

[4]Jean Janzen, *The Upside-Down Tree* (Winnipeg: Henderson Books, 1992),
31.

# 1
# Mud: The Mound That Saves Us

I begin with a poem which I wrote as a tribute to Rudy Wiebe for the "Mennonite/s Writing" conference in Goshen, Indiana, in 2002:

*Mud*

Our ancestors dug with their hands,
scooping tons of cold mud
to raise themselves above
the North Sea tides.
"They perch on these hummocks
with their children and animals
as though shipwrecked,"
wrote Pliny the Elder two millenia ago.

Like them you build a mound,
your hands scraped and sore
from the dig for words, one
after another, lift them
into story, naming who we are.
And you invite us to huddle there
with you, shivering and alive.

I stood on one of those mounds in Friesland in northern Holland in 1996, learning about the first Frisians, probably my people. Historians write that the Frisian tribes moved more earth than the Egyptians did for their pyramids. To get out of the floods and tides, they spent twelve centuries building *terps,* which are mounds of earth five to forty acres each, sometimes thirty feet high, building over one thousand of them. It is estimated that the Frisians moved 100,000,000 cubic yards of clay for no other reason than to raise themselves out of the water, while the Egyptians raised only one-third of that. The poet Rod Jellema writes, "The *terps* are not registered as one of the wonders of the world, but perhaps the stubbornness of the workers ought to be."[5] Mud mounds meant survival. I propose that this elemental material is a foundation of all good and faithful writing.

I also chose this poem to begin these chapters as a way to acknowledge that Rudy Wiebe's novels, especially *The Blue Mountains of China*,[6] were a major influence on my desire to write. His incisive and beautiful fiction challenged me like a mountain to write my family's history in an artistic way.

I wish to investigate three forms of mud as a saving mound for the writer: first, as source of nourishment; second, mud as cure for blindness; and third, mud as sacramental.

## Mud as Source of Nourishment

Land, earth, mud is central to our story as Mennonites. Our self-perception of our past and our present, for many of us, is tied to crops and seasons, to ownership of land. Those of us who grew up in small towns were only a short remove from the farm. Even in town we had vast gardens, a cow, some chickens, and sometimes sheep. Good soil meant food for a family of ten, harvested and preserved for the entire year. Gratitude for harvest was a church festival, a time to overflow in giving to MCC and missions.

Pleasure, nourishment, taste, and love are all intertwined, and become the subject of celebration in many poems. We think of Julia Kasdorf's references to food as cure. I have written about canning peaches and chickens, and about the wild grapes which my grandfather asked for on his deathbed. Food easily becomes metaphor, but is, in fact, what keeps us alive and writing. It is right to praise this gift from the earth, from our gracious God. "Eating ends the annual drama of the food economy that begins with planting and birth," writes Wendell Berry. To eat with fullest pleasure "is perhaps the profoundest enactment of our connection with the world," he continues. "In this pleasure we

---

[5]Rod Jellema, *The Sound That Remains* (Grand Rapids, Mich.: Eerdmans, 1990), xxxiii.

[6]Rudy Wiebe, *The Blue Mountains of China* (Toronto, Ont.: McClelland and Stewart, 1970).

experience and celebrate our dependence and our gratitude, for we are living from mystery, from creatures we did not make and powers we cannot comprehend." He then quotes lines by the poet William Carlos Williams: "There is nothing to eat,/seek it where you will,/but the body of the Lord."[7] I use these lines as an epigraph for my poem entitled "Table."

> Hen running in the field,
> her stunted wings spreading
> without lift or flight.
> And yet, the quick dance
> of her scratching claws.
>
> She raises a circle of dust,
> she settles into it.
> O Light of the world
> in every speck against
> every feather!
>
> O nourishing Fire
> in the crushed worm
> caught in her yellow bill
> and in this bright yolk
> on my plate.
>
> And from the blazing grass
> through the dark labyrinths
> of the cow, this butter,
> given in remembrance,
> melting for me.

With this poem I anticipate the third point of this talk that, like the crushed worm, mud is holy. At the same time I celebrate food for itself, as gift indeed. Our primary hunger is for food, and yet for humans this nourishment is inextricably bound with the need to be touched and held, kissed, and

---

[7] Wendell Berry, *What Are People For?* (San Francisco: North Point Press, 1990), 144, 152.

spoken to. Scott Holland, an Anabaptist theologian, writes that poets have been teaching him about the tongue as an organ of both language and taste. He goes on to describe a Eucharistic hunger underlying all our loves and losses.[8] As Duane Friesen writes, "Humans live by both bread and meaning. Like all animals, we must eat in order to survive. The meaning of our lives is expressed through eating rituals, such as the Lord's Supper or a Sabbath meal."[9] Food from the mud is an essential source for the writer.

The power of place has inspired poets through the ages. Nature, the flora and fauna, the changing topography of land. Wild and open spaces, cities, towns, oceans, rivers, and skies. We internalize outer landscapes and project inner ones. For me the power of landscape has resulted in poems about Saskatchewan, my birthplace, the midwest skies and fields of my childhood, and then the majestic California valley and mountain range of my adulthood.

Nature as metaphor has dominated much of my own poetry as well as the poems of many others. The nurture of nature and landscape has pushed me into the questions of wilderness and home. Some of those questions were evoked by the change from a landscape which seemed to be owned by people to a landscape which seems to own me. This evoked poems about loss of control, the demands of grandeur, and fear of getting lost in it, especially the mountains. And also, drowning in the magnificent ocean. Questions about the fertility of the valley in close proximity to the wildness of the mountains. Beauty and terror. And inevitably many writers are drawn to the connections between the aesthetic and the religious.

It has been informative for me to study the life and writings of the poet Czeslaw Milosz who moved to Berkeley, California, in the early sixties, about the same time that we moved to the

---

[8]Scott Holland, "Toward a Hermeneutics of the Gesture or Even the Postmodern Story Has a Body: Narrative, Poetry & Ritual," paper presented at "Ritual in Anabaptist Communities" conference, Hillsdale College, Michigan, June 26-28, 2003, p. 9.

[9]Duane K. Friesen, *Artists, Citizens, Philosophers: Seeking the Peace of the City* (Scottdale, Pa.: Herald Press, 2000), 67.

Central Valley. He comments that the European landscape can easily be imagined as humane, a stage for human strivings, shaped by human values. The American West does not permit such comforting delusions, and what immigrants see is "an alien and indifferent thing." He writes, "Now I seek shelter in these pages, but my humanistic zeal has been weakened by the mountains and the ocean, by those many moments when I have gazed upon boundless immensities with a feeling akin to nausea, the wind ravaging my little homestead of hopes and intentions." He quarrels with it and with Robinson Jeffers, whom he evaluates as a poet who deals with inhuman things. He concludes, "The only thing we can do is try to communicate with one another, our concrete presence, our uniqueness."[10]

My own experience with the mountains' nearness has moved me to try language. About what, I wasn't sure. And I am still investigating. Becoming more clear is the fact that the mountain is some of the most primal material on earth, perhaps most holy, and enigmatic. The biblical references are clear—it is the place for the temple, where Moses received the Law, where Jesus sat to teach. I haven't claimed the mountain as home, but a place to visit, to stand again in awe, looking at the range of Sierra, letting it teach me.

In my poem entitled "The Mountain," I describe taking our young children to the immensity of the mountain, to the river's great roar, and the granite walls which "stood taller than the world . . . This is home, we said,/ but they couldn't hear us." When we carried them back into their rooms, we recognized that we ourselves were in new spaces "that couldn't hold us now, but vibrated outward without end." The poem moves on to a description of the lush, green slopes of spring which lure us up to the "high meadow's chilled nightfall," and to "its granite lap" which is the "bed for us all." The child, distracted by small animals, may lose his way. Thus the mountain with its white peak seems to claim us for our final destination, and I ask,

---

[10]Leonard Nathan and Arthur Quinn, *The Poet's Work: An Introduction to Czeslaw Milosz* (Cambridge, Mass.: Harvard University Press, 1991), 3.

"Where is home? This place or the fertile valley?"[11] We hunger for both, and the mountain remains, silent and waiting.

Our bodies are a chief source of mud as nourishment for the writer. We come from earth. *Adama* means earthling, or clod of earth. Duane Friesen quotes Wolterstorff as one who grounds his theology of art in the notion of human beings as earthlings. Friesen affirms that we are God's finite creatures made of the physical stuff of the universe, and therefore called to affirm the beauty of the human body, of sexual love, and the longing to love each other genuinely. The writer "must have a profound respect for the material stuff of the universe and engage in an intimate dialogue with it."[12] Poetry is about being a body, not in a body, separate from spirit. Job, the Psalms, the Song of Solomon are full of body and earth. And so are the Gospels.

Much of my own poetry has found its source in the body. The womanly experience of loving, giving birth, nurturing, and ageing is centered in the body. Writing about my sexuality raised the eyebrows of a few, but was more often acknowledged as a necessary corrective in the Mennonite community. "Would you call yourself the Mennonite sex poet?" a student asked me at Eastern Mennonite University when I first read my poems there. And I heard recently that some Goshen students pinned up my poem, "I keep forgetting that flowers/are sexual organs," in the dorm, and how shocked they were to meet me and see that I was as old, or older, than their mothers.

Acknowledging the body has been liberating for me. Honoring it as part of the spiritual journey, in fact, inextricably entwined, has allowed deeper connections to earth, and the cosmos. We long for an embodied theology. And we thrive in the wonder of being part of the cosmos, like all human beings. "The cells that make our bodies work came to birth in processes that began billions of years ago. We are united in God with all humanity and with all beings, from the stars of the heavens to the earth, the air, the trees, and the tiniest particles of the universe."[13] I am quoting Duane Friesen again.

---

[11]*Tasting the Dust*, 12.
[12]Friesen, 199.
[13]Friesen, 24.

We are mud. We are dependent on it. To write from that perspective, to sit before the empty page with that recognition is the foundation. It is repeatedly the place of humility and survival.

## Mud as Cure for Blindness

Speaking of the body, isn't it interesting that the healing of the blind man in the Gospels involved a mix of Jesus' spit and dirt? How elemental indeed. If you don't have water, you use spit. And what a fine example of the incarnation. In the following poem you will catch the reference to the healing story.

*The Clarity of Dirt*

A woman sits by late lamplight
planting violets on bonnets
with her needle. Today she pressed
sheets and pillowcases, white

with roses on the borders. Soon
the harvesters will come in.
Too exhausted to wash,
they will lie down on those

linens, the dirt making prints
of their bodies. And they
will dream with a certain clarity.
Like the blind man with mud

on his eyes, they will see trees
walking like men. They will
rise up to meet them, lifting
their loads easily, as in

a dance. And she will dream
that the meadow has come into
her house, that she is floating
on it, her children running

> freely with muddy feet
> over her sheeted body. All of them
> in this night-darkened house
> knowing in their sleep
>
> why they are here, what they
> were meant to be.[14]

The reference to "trees walking like men" is a deliberate reversal. Earth and the cleanliness of home become intertwined; we are part of earth, and it is part of us. Mud is a cure for the longing to be separate, to avoid our humanness. Not that the beautiful embroidered linens are without value, but they exist for the muddy body to lie upon and be healed, to dream the true dream.

This is a call to write the concrete mud-language of life, and to avoid a reliance on abstractions. Real images are the stuff of all good literature, including the Bible. "Go in fear of abstractions," advised poet Ezra Pound. Particulars are proof-positive in a way that abstractions cannot be. William Carlos Williams' famous dictum, "No ideas but in things," does not mean no ideas; rather it means ideas arrived at, universals discovered through particulars. Again it is the earthly that saves us from the overstatement of abstractions and their tendency to blow away like clouds, or to blind the imagination to any further consideration.

In the "Clarity of Dirt" I infer the deeper meaning of becoming dirty. I think of it as the way to salvation. I "know in my sleep" why I am here, what I was "meant to be." The children running over my sheeted body could be reference to death, but I see it as a giving of myself to life and love in the most basic sense of the words. I have been saved by the meadow, the earth, the earthiness of me.

Nice Mennonite girls didn't fall in the mud. Dena Pence Frantz, a Brethren theologian and my former pastor, refers to the struggle of girls with the concept of salvation. We act as if the Fall never happened, and we are afraid to fall, to fail. Boys

---

[14]*The Upside-Down Tree*, 23.

more often were allowed to get dirty. But the Fall has already happened; we will not cause it by our failures. We are human and dirty and loved by God who came to us as a baby in a cave among animals. Mud is a cure for blindness.

This cure necessarily includes our presence as humans in community, living together in the real territory, in a physical region. This is the place which Wendell Berry calls tragic, because it involves the need to survive mortality, partiality, and evil. It the place where we are cured of selfishness and can learn forgiveness of human nature and human circumstance.[15]

## Mud as Sacramental

Teilhard de Chardin wrote this: "Plunge into matter. Plunge into God. By means of all created things, without exception, the divine assails us, penetrates us, and molds us. We imagined it as distant and inaccessible, whereas in fact we live steeped in its burning layers."[16] He writes about the Cosmic Christ, the one who inhabits all. The Word became flesh and dwelt among us. This is where writing begins—incarnation, words putting on flesh in the presence of the Cosmic Christ. The faithful writer enters the nourishing soil of life with all its brokenness, pain, betrayals, as well as its faithful lovings, its glories, its fruits. We are part of the Great Comedy, Christ becoming flesh, dying and resurrecting, breaking the familiar, seasonal round, opening the doors to a life empowered by that event.

Scott Holland, in his encouragement of the arts, writes about aesthetics coming before ethics. In his work as preacher, teacher, and writer, he has attempted to return to the wonder of a sacramental universe through the reminder that God is revealed not only through the spiritual proclamation of the word, but also in the carnal manifestation of the world. He reminds us that the word became flesh, but the flesh becomes word again and again.

---

[15]Berry, 71-87.

[16]Annie Dillard, *For the Time Being* (New York: Vintage Books, 1999), 171.

Some Anabaptist thinkers have separated church from culture and creation, and think of only community as sacramental. Not earth, water, fire, or wind. Not body, breath, bread, or wine. For them, God inhabits ethics, not earth. But the early Anabaptists, Holland argues, were suspicious of an established sacramental system that domesticated the wildness of the elements for "narrow religious, political and economic ends."[17] God transcends the official and orthodox readings of church, culture, and creation. "Because body and breath were born from the primordial art of earth and spirit, not metaphysics, may I suggest that in the ecology of true spirituality, aesthetics must precede ethics because the grand story of creation precedes the story of the church?" he asks. "Because there is sin in the holy sanctuary and grace in the fallen world, we need a theology as large as life, a theology of church, culture, and creation."[18]

The faithful writer digs, word by word, for the clearest portrayal of what it means to become truly human as Christ showed us. It is a holy task. In humility, writers can be part of the continuing creation of the world. We are part of the primal material. God is not finished with us.

In the poem "Night Falls on the Neighborhood" I reflect on a painting by my son, Peter Janzen, a night scene of a street of suburban houses which seem to me to be locked and separate. "Nothing is revealed." Only in our "first deep sleep" do we hear "the secret/ of the neighborhood—/ that we all ride/ earth's original music" and that we are bound together in this ongoing work of God's creation. "God's brooding still hovers/ over us."[19]

The challenge to the writer is to reclaim the land. Build the mound to avoid being drowned by a tendency to separate from the real stuff of life. Reclaim the wonder of the gifts of earth, the nourishment of the places we inhabit, the food and beauty

---

[17]Scott Holland, "Reflections on Water," *Kairos: Arts and Letters of the Mennonite Culture* 2:1 (spring/summer 1997): 6-7.

[18]Scott Holland, "Experience," *Kairos: Arts and Letters of the Mennonite Culture* 1:2 (fall/winter 1996-97): 5.

[19]Jean Janzen, *Piano in the Vineyard* (Intercourse, Pa.: Good Books, 2004), 56.

of the land. Stay with the digging, stubbornly building a place for greater illumination and vision. Reclaim the mound as home: this earth, this mud, is who and what we are. Reclaim the mystery and holiness as you investigate "what lies hidden."

# 2
# Water: Wailing in the Shower

I began with the element of mud. I chose "mud" over "earth" because of my interest in our Dutch history and the amazing reclamation of land, which was mud. Because earth cannot be mud without water, it seemed natural to move to the element of water. All four elements could arguably be the first, all of them essential to sustain and bring life. But certainly water is primal. We are born out of water, and while our mouths open for air in our first cries, we soon need to drink more water to live. A high percentage of our bodies is water.

These chapters are a call for writers to reclaim the elements for the way they teach us to be faithful in naming who we really are. I choose the title "Wailing in the Shower" because it introduces the essential need we have to give voice to our experience. I share with you a naming story.

When our son Peter was a freshman in college, he came home with two Michaels, both becoming his best friends in the first weeks. I asked how they would tell each other apart, would one be Mike? No, we are both Michaels, they insisted. So I asked about last names—Gunther and Swartzendruber. We have few Swartzendrubers in California, so I was curious. I know that "swartz" means black in German, but I don't know what "druber" means. "My father told me it means grapes," said Michael S. "Oh, you have come to the heaven of black grapes," I replied. "This valley in September has the biggest, sweetest black grapes in the world. Come over for Sunday dinner, and we will have some with the meal." Both Michaels came and were enjoying the roast beef and the grapes when Michael Gunther asked, "Do you know what Gunther means? It means white angel food cake with whipped cream." To name is to love.

Water with its lifegiving flow is emblematic of our life experience. Writers try to find language to give name to this one amazing and fleeting life which we are given to live. I offer the poem "Wailing in the Shower" as an example of this attempt:

After the elation of giving birth,
our new daughter fed and sleeping,
I stand under the warm flow
and begin on the high notes—
Madame Butterfly's ecstasy,
"One fine day in May," the water's
harmony sliding over my body.

*

After the loss of his bride,
our friend turns on the guestroom shower
and begins his long wailing.
It echoes throughout the house,
flows down the stairway,
his baritone cries rising and falling.
Over and over, the full octaves of pain.

*

This narrow passage
from birth to death,
like lines of song on a page,
our first wail carrying us
on breath and air toward
the final water.
Butterfly bows as far as she can. Her son
is that small figure waving
goodbye, and behind him
is the shining bay blinding our eyes.[20]

   Some of us begin our day in the shower, and some of us sing in the shower. When I describe my own ecstatic singing after the birth of our daughter, I don't tell you about the hospital housekeeper who came running, breathless, to see if I was okay. She thought I was screaming. This melody is famous for the beauty of expectation, Butterfly preparing for her lover to

---

[20]*Piano in the Vineyard*, 19.

return to her from America. This water song is one of great desire and longing. It returns us to our place of origin, our own births. The wonder of our own existence.

Water also is primal in its flow, the constant reminder that we are born into flow, into time. And that that time ends. Our friend who is wailing for the loss of his bride becomes an emblem of all losses. He could not remain silent. Perhaps he thought that the running water would drown out his sobs, while in fact the shower acted as an acoustic shell. I will never forget how helpless I felt as I listened. I was changed by his great weeping, a kind of baptism of loss.

In the poem's final section I refer to the song of life, that flow which starts and stops. Butterfly learns that her lover has married an American wife and will take her son with them because she does not have other resources for his care. In her despair she kneels and kills herself with a knife, "bowing as far as she can." The little boy on stage waves from a distance as he leaves, and the last, tragic chords of Puccini's opera fill the world. But the bay is shining; the boy has a future. In the Japanese culture Butterfly's method of death can be thought of as honorable. We feel this huge sense of tragedy mixed with the glimmer of hope that her life will continue through her son.

This is the power of song. This is the power of words that are sung. This is my call to you to drink the water of this holy earth. You can do this by immersing yourself in the great writings and songs of human experience, our world's literature, in the sacred writings of our Scriptures, the Psalms and Prophets, and the astounding Gospels. And this is an invitation to you to write your own stories and poems, to make your own art, to be a faithful witness. Immerse yourself. Water is an essential element of the faithful writer.

I invite you to listen to my poem entitled "Lakes." It is written in five short sections, the first three based on the memory of a lake of my childhood in Mountain Lake, Minnesota. The other two are set in Austria and California.

*Lakes, part 1*

Every Sunday as we drove past,
it was a different thing—
a plate of porcelain, thick,
under which fish moved,
searching; a keyhole
shimmering, waiting
for the swinging door;
or a mirror glaring so that
I was blinded
unless I turned away
just enough to catch
a glimpse of the real.
Always it was a glimpse
until I entered it,
until one day
I felt the stones
under my feet,
the slimy grass waving,
and the water lifting me.

Childhood is like the mystery of collected water, this lake
which I could view from the top of the hill as our family car
descended on the road to the little Valley Church. The lake
changed; it was ice with fish movement underneath; it was a
shimmering keyhole to something great and amazing; it was a
mirror too bright to look at directly. This is about wonder,
about the intuitive sense that the physical is more than itself.
Our imaginations are a sacred gift. And this section affirms the
primal importance of the real as grounding our imaginations. All
we imagine means little, or rarely changes us, unless we allow
ourselves to enter and feel the stones and the grass, the water
lifting us. Good writing keeps us connected to reality. The
physical and the spiritual are not separate.

*Lakes, part 2*

Sometimes we would picnic
above the lake on the high
slope, girls together.

We wove crowns of dandelions,
our limbs and laughter light,
and yet we felt a pull under the grass.

Somehow we knew, at ten
and eleven, the weight
of water and its demands,

so that the lake below us
became ours—the way
it kept its arms open

and filled, the way
it would feed the hidden
spaces waiting beneath it.

The weight of water, the weight of experience. Girls anticipating womanhood, birthgiving, loving selflessly, the water's demands of time and death. All of it underneath, pulling. And for me, writing this as an adult, I add the weight of knowing the 20th century, the wars, the bodies piled up, the stories of my uncles and aunts starving to death in Stalinist Soviet Union. And the weight of joy as well, what is given in the rhythm of seasons, in companionship, in laughter, and in loving.

The open arms of the lake, the hidden spaces waiting, infers the uncertainty of the future. So much is unpredictable and complex. As the poet Milosz writes, life is polyphonic. This Nobel Prize winning poet, who survived the horrors of Gdansk, Poland, in the 30s, whose inquiries about life and his traditional faith are tortured and honest, finds light in the writings of Dostoevsky. He sees that the writer cannot resolve humanist skepticism and religious faith.

Faith is only a voice among many, but he will find affirmations in spite of the skepticism, a purifying sense of "ambivalent laughter." He will call himself an "ecstatic pessimist."[21]

Like Milosz the faithful writer recognizes multiplicity and layers. The music of the writing, therefore, is truer and richer. As readers we enter the human dilemmas of the quest. We enter the struggle for faith.

*Lakes, part 3*

When my father baptized
the teenage girls, they wore white
and walked in one by one.
His starched shirt sleeves softened
as he lifted the lake into their hair.
And they walked out one by one,
sloshing against the heaviness,
their dresses clinging to their hips,
their bare feet gathering
the muddy sand, as the trinity
shone in their hair, which they
kept bound until bedtime,
when it fell around their bare
shoulders, and filled the shadows
of their rooms.

This is water as the place of ritual, of choice, and of change. This reflects the rivers and lakes of the bible, of healing, and of entry into the promised land. And it is about love. Here my father is performing the ritual of baptism. He is blessing girls who are older than me and ready. I am full of longing and desire to be one of them, and yet hesitant because of the implications of binding, of purity, and of being immersed in the demands and holiness of God. Here too is the necessity to give language to the body—the wet clothing against the hips, the wet hair. Sensuality and spirituality become one.

---

[21]Nathan and Quinn, 101.

*Lakes, part 4*

Never had we floated on such clarity as on the Königsee,
a liquid diamond holding us
high in the Alps.
Only a faint ripple, as when we
barely breathe, our bodies
an interruption of depth
and stillness, our eyes burning,
our hands dipping into that light,
so cold and pure, we knew
that only a mountain could hold it.

The faithful writer will record experiences of ecstasy as he bears witness. Ecstasy holds the sense of the unexplainable, the mystery. Often our experience with nature brings together the aesthetic and religious. We sense the power and terror of beauty; we know that these experiences could change our lives. Duane Friesen writes that "we live in the tension between our experience of finitude and of transcendence."[22] We seek language for this.

*Lakes, part 5*

Each spring we find Lost Lake
again, thickening with horsetail
and dragonflies. And every year
our children bring their nets.
Where nothing moved in the heat
of last August, they now join
the blur of spring; all afternoon
they splash and call.
So that at dusk, when they enter
the car, the lost is held in their skin,

---

[22]Friesen, 204.

in the swinging of their limbs, and in
the wings battering against the sides of the jar.[23]

Like my children catching butterflies at Lost Lake, the reader
is invited to enter into all that is in motion, new life caught in a
poem or story, making it part of your own journey of discovery.
You are the one holding the net. You are the one noticing,
being active, capturing it in your very skin, what might have
been lost in this amazing life.

The dilemma remains—the butterfly in the jar will die if you
keep it there. And so you catch, observe, and give it back to the
world in a new form. What is the responsibility of the writer?
To make it as true and as memorable as you can, borrowing as
we all do and must from the great writers of the past, and
making it our own and new.

The water of the earth is old; it has been here from the
creation of the universe. It is only as new as it is recirculated.
And it is always changing, in motion. Sometimes it is the roar
and rush of river or the ocean. Even in the quiet lake the air lifts
it into mist, changing it. We are only able to capture the
moment. And yet, water with its various properties of river
rush, of soft and hard rain, snow and ice, becomes a powerful
metaphor over and over again. We go back to it for the way it
offers itself, changeable and momentary as it is.

Here is a quote from Terry Tempest Williams: "We are water.
We are swept away. Desire begins in wetness. (We are) born out
of longing, wet, not dry. We can always return to our place of
origin. Water. Water Music. We are baptized by immersion,
nothing less can replenish or restore our capacity to love. It is
endless if we believe in water."[24]

Scott Holland reminds us that in the Genesis creation
narrative we read how *ruach*—the breath, wind, or spirit of God
moved over the waters. The waters of baptism flow from these
vast waters of all creation. These waters unite us with the
creation and the cosmos. They unite us to love. We are saved by

---

[23]*Tasting the Dust*, 54.
[24]Terry Tempest Williams, quoted by Holland, "Reflections on Water,"
6.

water and word, the Gospel teaches. "Creativity is endless if we really believe in water."[25] It is from this primal source that we seek language for the great themes of faithful writing.

As I looked through my body of poems, I was surprised to find more water poems than I expected. The collections are really quite damp, and that may be a reflection on the fact that I live in a dry, subtropical area, with no rain for six months of the year. During those times we depend on the mountain snows coming down in creeks and canals for irrigation. In the poem "At Summer's End" I meditate on the "slow drain/ into silence" which I experience each fall as I walk beside the dying creek, a deprivation which allows me to see what has been "lost and discarded." Our secrets are no longer carried away to the sea. Sometimes the drowned are finally found because "that green music . . . has to stop," which is a gift, and which is the truth of our own ending.[26]

The writer probes the primal material for the mysteries, the questions of beginnings and endings, and sometimes for the source of language itself. In the poem "Glocken" I began with a very early childhood memory, my father tipping tubs of snow into a hole in our kitchen floor. This was in Saskatchewan where I was born on a wintry day and lived my first five years. The winter outside was a "wide silence," "muffled" and "hushed." But inside when the snow was dumped into "the black cistern under the floor,/ I heard the echoing plunk, plunk,/ of what lay beneath us." In the next stanza I assert, "Something waits to stir,/ to make its dark music," recalling how my young son coming out of a febrile seizure sang "Kling, Glocken, kling-aling-aling/ in a voice high and clear, a bell/ in a language he didn't know."[27]

The writer listens for what is buried deeply, for the mystery of language itself, and the power of the sound. Some of the subjects for writing seem to be buried, and we have to dig.

---

[25]Holland, "Reflections on Water," 6-7.

[26]*Tasting the Dust*, 15.

[27]Jean Janzen, *Snake in the Parsonage* (Intercourse, Pa.: Good Books, 1995), 35.

Sometimes the shimmering world lies before us, offering itself. And always the senses are primal.

You have language, sources from childhood, and ongoing experience. How do you keep going, and why? What sustains the faithful writer? I offer you my poem, "Flowers of Amsterdam," as holding some of the images which I have found to express my own journey into that question. Since Amsterdam is a city of canals, it is associated with this primal element, its houses leaning toward water, reflected in water, its origins dependent on water travel. Amsterdam, part of our early Mennonite history, city of flowers and great art.

*Flowers of Amsterdam*

For the sake of the Gospel,
the book says. 1549. Pieter, Johann
and Barbara are tied to the stake.
Their bodies flare out in a triple bloom,
still flare out in the mind, the recalcitrant
flesh still acrid. And Catherine drowns
in the canal, her skirts billowing out
over her tied legs like a lily.

Now vast markets of flowers, a harbor
where once a shipload of grain
was exchanged for a single tulip bulb.
City of night when the streets open
their black laps for the painted blooms,
when music rides the blue and swollen veins,
washed and languid houses that double
in the watery streets.

City of choices. Which fire, which perfume,
and at what price? Catherine cries out
over the water. Each one must choose,
each one for himself. And how
do you choose when a whirlpool sucks you in,
into the purple corridors of the iris,
the cool swarm of apple orchards?
"Careful of the feast's tomorrow," Van Gogh
writes near the end, after the yellow skies.
"For my own work I am risking my life,
and my mind is half-gone. . . But what do you want?"

What do you want? The one way to live,
the one unequivocal rose in this life
of mirrors, in this city of water where
the day is now nearly gone and the floodgates
already open. The dark elms dip their hair
into the rising tide and the laden boats
drift with the current. But here and there
one moves against it, one figure in a boat,
the twin oars quietly opening the water's
glistening petals, opening a secret passage
in the deep and watery place.[28]

The Gospel sustains with its demands and assurances, its call to loyalty. This kind of passion and martyrdom seems far away and long ago, and yet it is part of our world today. The wailing of repentance and ecstasy of adherence is real even now. Bearing witness to our culture's pain and darkness is part of our continuing call, to name and give voice to injustice, sin, and loss. To name the beauty of this world, its fire and perfume, its color, is a sustaining call. But most intense of all is the longing to know how to live this life, and to find what is secret and hidden, which pulls us to the deep and watery places. This is the life of the writer, to continue that restless inquiry, and to find, if not the secrets, the connections which make life more whole.

---

[28]*The Upside-Down Tree*, 34.

What kind of life is that? How can one find support for such a journey? Whether you become a writer or not, all choices can seem immense; the world's chaos threatens, the needs seem overwhelming, and nothing is secure. Enter the water with confidence. God is with you, our loving God of the vast cosmos, and as near as our hands and breath. I wish to end this challenge with a poem of affirmation:

*Before Sleep*

All day the ocean asked
the same questions.
There at the edge of the cliff
where the car doors flew open,
our children spilled out to play,
to scramble wet rocks in high wind,
and at times we lost sight of them.
Today among the roar the gray whales
breached and blew northward,
their calves following close.
A child of the plains, I couldn't imagine
these glittering fields
or that rise of slippery mass
above them. Again and again
we asked each other, "Did you see,"
and followed their spouts until
they disappeared into the dusk.
The limestone hollows echoed
as the water pulled away
from the cliffs, and we returned
to our room where last night
we saw the moon hang her sickle-light
over the high breakers
as we stood arm in arm.
Were they ready for this undertow,
those endless miles of shine,
this wind that drenches
the leaning cypresses? Those dark bodies
tumble northward as our own fall

into drowsiness, and we ride once again
our mother's heartbeat, serene
in her steerage. Her lungs fill
and empty over me, and tonight
I think I hear her singing.[29]

God is present in the waters of the world—the lakes, rivers, and oceans. Water of great power to change the shape of the land, and quiet water for our meditation. We ride on it, swim in it, flow with it, drink it. Water is life for the writer.

---

[29]*The Upside-Down Tree*, 26.

# 3
## Fire and Air: Breathing the Light

Garrison Keillor's latest book is a collection of poems selected from the ones he has read on his daily five-minute show "The Writer's Almanac," which airs on public radio.[30] These are poems, he says, that can make people "stop chewing their toasted muffins and turn up the radio." The range extends from classics to a host of delightful contemporary poems. The *Christian Century* recently interviewed Keillor about the poems in Lake Wobegon and in his anthology. The interviewer comments on the section titled "O Lord," and asks him about the gratitude which is common in those poems. He answers that gratitude is where spiritual life begins. "Thank you for this amazing and bountiful life and forgive us if we do not love it enough." He thanks for the laptop computer and for the yellow kitchen table and for the clock on the wall and for the coffee and the black slacks and his black T-shirt. "Thanks for black, and for the other colors, and for giving me the wherewithal not to fix a half-pound cheeseburger right now and to eat a stalk of celery instead." He goes on, and suggests that we begin every day with this exercise of enumerating one's blessings and set them before the Lord. "It is to break through the thin membrane of sourness and sullenness, though we should be thankful for that too, it being the source of so much wit and humor."

The interviewer then asks, "Are there other categories of 'religious' poems you might include if you were to put together another volume?" "Yes, I'd put in a section of confessional poems. True confession is extremely rare in poetry, as in life. When a poet pretends to confess, usually he does it in a pretty heroic manner: 'Forgive me Lord, that I have foolishly bestowed love on these raving idiots.' You seldom hear someone cop to the real basic stuff: 'Forgive me, Lord, for being this self-righteous prick and walking around with a mirror held up in front of my face. Relieve me, Lord, of this stupid self-consciousness, this absolutely insufferable ego. God, it is making me miserable. I lust after recognition, I am desperate to

---

[30]Garrison Keillor, *Good Poems* (New York: Viking, 2002).

win all the little merit badges and trinkets of my profession, and I am of less real use in this world than any good cleaning lady. I have written reams of high-falutin' nonsense and it is nothing but fishwrap and a dog's biffy.' You don't get this kind of honesty often from writers, and of course it ought to be encouraged. Scripture tells us to confess our sins to each other, and I wish that the poets I know would do this more often. They could use a little more humility, frankly. We humorists can't do the whole job alone."[31]

I begin this third chapter based on the elements of faithful writing with a poem which is a gratitude poem, one which celebrates air and light as found in the common and ordinary acts of life. It's a kitchen poem, that nourishing center of the home. (The confession poem comes later.)

> Vermeer had it right, I think,
> the woman with the jug, a common
> kitchen, the light.
>
> Farther south, angels erupted
> in lightning skies, saints rose
> on clouds, mothers strained their arms
> upward, their eyes wild.
>
> Oh, I know, when my child lies dying,
> I want the breakthrough. And those days
> when everything scrapes and pulls
> me down, and yet,
>
> the simple rituals of the house,
> the washing up, the kneading, the rising,
> the jug of water holding the day's
> light. The miracle of air.[32]

---

[31]Garrison Keillor, "Wobegon Poets," *Christian Century*, March 22, 2003, p. 21.
[32]*The Upside-Down Tree*, 40.

Watery, muddy Holland, and yet, that light, that air. Air as life, what keeps us here and breathing. The wind as power and force for change. Fire as the source of all, the original energy, creating, generative, the source of light. I choose to reflect on air and fire together because I see the writing process energized by that combination, that the life of the writer is sustained by breathing the light.

One of the answers which we give to those who ask, why do you write, is this: "I want to see what I am thinking." The tasks of the writer are exploration, asking the right questions (digging in the mud), bearing witness to life experience (water), and examining the interior life and its relation to experience. The writer seeks the unity of this complex life of being human. I will reflect on four characteristics of this seeking, this breathing of air and light: a willingness to take risks, a willingness to persevere in the work, an openness to incorporation of history and tradition, and recognition of the transcendent. To give some order to this diffusion of air and fire, I have chosen to go to the master painter of light, Johannes Vermeer, and comment on the poems which look at his paintings of women who stand in window light. I chose four of these as division poems in my collection *Tasting the Dust.*

*Window Facing South*

"Young Girl with Water Pitcher" Vermeer

Caught in the motion
of opening the window,
she is held in uncertainty—
was that a voice rising

from the street, or someone
calling to her within the house?
One hand on the brass pitcher,
the other on the window latch,

she is suspended in the air
of spring which has filled
the room, ready to loosen
whatever is bound.[33]

This southern exposure to the light of spring, as I imagine it, suggests warmth and fertility, the opening of the world into blossom, and the opening of this adolescent girl. Her stance and expression is a mix of hesitation and desire. She is suspended. She is waiting. Should she stay, should she go outside to join what is becoming loosened and unbound? This is the quest for life and creativity, of discovery. The girl holds a source of life, water, the weight of her responsibility in life to give-and serve. But I see her wondering how that will be for her—only inside the safety of the house, the community. Or will she dare to move outside?

The faithful writer dares to ask, to go outside, to discover, and then to speak out. Breaking the silence has been one of the phrases used for the results of that risk. It is a first act of courage to simply describe truthfully what one sees and experiences, not with the expected response, but often the unexpected. The light of spring allows this, this symbol of longing and desire for new life. It is that light and air which allowed me to write about the suicide of my grandmother, about my fierce maternal love, the demands of marriage, and my longing for the presence of God in my life and in our world.

Early in my writing life, which began late, at the age of 47, I dreamed that I was driving our big station wagon alone, and I lost control at the edge of a steep cliff, tumbling down to a rough ocean beach. I climbed out alive and scrambled up the side, only to find the cliff's edge crumbling as I tried to cling to it with my hands. Above me, looking down, were my high school friends from my home church in Mountain Lake. They looked and began a discussion on whether I was spiritual enough to be worthy of rescue. I pleaded, and at last they pulled me up, took me into their motel room, but kept away from me, whispering, glancing. I had risked too much. I had crossed a

---

[33]*Tasting the Dust*, 3.

line. How daring, how true to life, myself, and God could I be? Would I have to say with Huck Finn, "Alright, then I'll go to hell!" I had lived a life of trying to please everyone; now I was testing the waters of telling the truth with poetry.

The poems that follow this poem of youth and longing are mostly poems about the California landscape, and the demands of the wilderness, especially the mountains. Life is huge, life ends, much waits to be celebrated and feasted upon. There is healing in the fruit of the orange tree. Always for the artist and writer, there is new territory to explore, and that requires risk.

The second window faces north. The light is pale and rather cold.

*Window Facing North*

"Maidservant Pouring Milk" Vermeer

She will spend her lifetime
in rooms, confined
to bread, table, wool,

and a narrow stream of milk.
Long tables of guests wait
somewhere, her children bang spoons

against their empty bowls,
and what she was given is
a rough pitcher, a window,

bread, and an apron
which grows deeper
in the folds of indigo blue,

all of it held
in a pale morning light,
her whole body pouring.[34]

---

[34]*Tasting the Dust*, 17.

This maid servant will pour milk for hundreds of years, and still the light shines out of the milk, the pitcher, bread, her apron, her face. She will stay in the room; she will serve and serve. The poems following this poem are about the work of writing and making art. I have poured milk for fifty years, literally, but I have been pouring poems for over twenty of those years. I have found that it is necessary to speak, to cry out. "Our stories are too big, for our bodies. Our first heartbeat/is spillover, and we are born/in a rush of water and cries. /With our whole body we lift/our first vowels to the air—/a stream pressing from a place we do not know."[35] The writer acknowledges the gift of language given early in life, as well as the limitations of words. We acknowledge faith in the endurance of what we write down, and faith that there is light, a deeper order, and great wonder. The faithful writer serves in winter light. The peaceful light in the face of the maid pouring milk can be the result of such labor.

*Window Facing East*

"Woman in Blue Reading a Letter" Vermeer

The landscape comes to her
in a room where she waited, where now
she stands beside two empty chairs,

table, and map, gripping the folded
page with both hands. The message
is a mountain range with valleys,

fields, and inscrutable lakes
vibrating against the page.
All this in one voice.

Now he is present in her face,
in the color blue,
the silk of her jacket,

---

[35]*Tasting the Dust*, 18.

and the chairs of stretched
leather, holding the shadows.[36]

The light in that room is soft and mysterious, probably not the dawn. But the woman faces east, which in religious tradition, is toward the return of Christ, the great coming dawn. The poem suggests that this is a letter from the beloved as he is present in her face and even in the color and texture of her jacket. And in the empty chairs. The absent one can be present in writing. We can be present to others with our writing.

But this could also be emblematic of the air and light of all writing which nurtures us, the literature of the past and present, the lives and thoughts of those who have entered the rich world of becoming authors. As a reader I sit in my physical space absorbing the world elsewhere and from another time. This is the hope of our attempts to communicate, to be a part of the recorded history of people in this world. My own poems in this section explored the landscape and history of Holland, our own Mennonite heritage there, and responses to Dutch art. I then moved to Italy, to the air and light of Siena, Venice, and Fra Angelico's frescoes.

In an essay entitled "The Responsibility of the Poet," Wendell Berry writes that a poem has the power to remind poet and reader alike of things they have read and heard. It has the power to remind them of things they have have not read and heard, but that have been read and heard by others whom they have read and heard. "Thus the art, so private in execution, is also communal and filial. . . . Any poem worth the name is the product of a convocation. It exists, literally by recalling past voices into presence."[37]

As faithful writers we borrow the story from others. We are nurtured by their lives and words. This light of communication and dialogue is the light of love, of desire and longing for the other. This is the air of life.

---

[36]*Tasting the Dust*, 35.
[37]Berry, 88, 89.

*Window Facing West*

"Lady Weighing Gold" Vermeer

Late afternoon
in a shadowed room,
the only light, her body

and the glint of pearls.
She has turned her back
to the painting on the wall—

The Last Judgment, black and blurred.
Nor is the judgment in her hands,
the scales balancing.

It rests in her calm face,
her delicate wrists,
her skin holding the light.

This poem risks a "new theology." When I say that the judgment is not in the woman's hands, or in the scales balancing, but in her skin, I am reaching for that elemental light, which is love, which is mercy. She is not a body with a separate spirit, but she holds the light of God in her skin. It was fascinating to me, when this collection was published, to see this poem facing the last poem of part three, in which Jesus forbids Mary Magdalene to touch his skin, and yet, I say, he wants to touch her. Skin on skin.

The fire of sorrow and loss enters these final poems. The air claims my mother's last breaths in "its reckless burning, this air/which we have borrowed since our first stunned gasp." And her bruises "flare in the dark."[38] I end this collection with reference to the fire that created the mountain, out of which my husband creates his garden as its soil and vegetation and water comes down to our valley.

---

[38]*Tasting the Dust*, 62.

The writer who breathes the light is invited to enter the world of risk and exploration, maybe even go into the wilderness. The writer of fire and air offers nourishment by her labor, absorbing the large legacy of what has been recorded. And the writer in the face of death holds the light of God in her skin.

How does the writer breathe the light? What is the language of fire and air? In the poem "The Language of Light" I meditate on that subject in three parts. In the first part I acknowledge that the artists in Holland in the 1600s grew "weary of war," and instead "lifted the slow fire/ of pewter onto canvas, the wild silk/ of tulips." They represented "heroism in the texture/ of brick, fine wool, copper gleam,/ and a housewife's face, open/ as a waterlily... In this watery country where light/ cannot be divided from light... earth itself holds light."[39] The fire is in the paint and in the threads of the canvas. The form and its particulars shine.

Light is in the form of the poem when its integrity reminds us of the formal integrity of other works, creatures, and structures of the world. Berry writes, "By its form it alludes to other forms, evokes them, resonates with them, and so becomes a part of the system of analogies or harmonies by which we live. Thus the poet affirms and collaborates in the formality of the Creation." He concludes, "This, I think, is a matter of supreme and mostly unacknowledged importance."[40]

In the second part I explore the language of music. The Dutch carillon spills "its barrels of tones around us... all their dark hollows/ bright now and falling."

> They pour over the brass scales,
> bright hats, and piled circles
> of Edam and Gouda, as if measurement
>
> and order are not complete
> without this wild joy
> which now enters me, finding

---

[39]*Tasting the Dust*, 36.
[40]Berry, 89.

a hidden place where light
has waited all my life,
ripe and ready to ring.[41]

Fire and air are present in music, and in this poem are celebrated in the sound and wild vibration of bells. The music of language is elemental. Wendell Berry articulates this well: "Fundamentally the technical means of poetry rests in its power as speech or song—the play of line against syntax and against stanza; the play of variation against form and against theme; the play of phrase against line, and of phrase against phrase within the line; the play of likenesses and differences of sounds; the play of statement with and against music; the play of rhyme against rhythm and as rhythm; the play of the poem as a made thing with and within and against the histories—personal and literary, national and local—that produce it."[42] This is the language of light. Within us are hidden places where we wait for this wild joy.

In part three I tell the story of Boniface, the missionary who arrived in Friesland in 1775 "slopping through the mud/ with the Book in his hands./ I stand on the mound where/ my frightened ancestors murdered him."[43] The language of light lived on in books and portraits of people reading the Bible, and in Haarlem in 1557 where a bookseller is martyred. The light we breathe is the Gospel recorded in the Book and carried through mud and murder. It is not possible to kill it. It is the hunger to know and the willingness to write it down. It is the beginning of the world and it is the "I" who made it with love, and who is love. This light is from the original fire.

How do we breathe this light when we write? "A good poem reminds us of love because it cannot be written or read in distraction; it cannot be written or understood by anyone thinking of praise or publication. . . . It is amateur work, lover's work." Again, Berry is helpful here. A poem is

---

[41]*Tasting the Dust*, 37.
[42]Berry, 88.
[43]*Tasting the Dust*, 38.

original, he writes, when it originates authentic feeling, when it claims attention and respect. The work is original in responding to its original source and by the just language and just music, and in that way charges the language with meaning.[44]

The original fire of creation, of love, of the Gospel, and of truth is what we long for as artists and writers. Sometimes that means destruction of what exists. Fire and wind can mean cleansing and regeneration. This is where confession comes in. This is the wild love which destroys for the sake of the new. We know deep within ourselves that we cannot save ourselves, that this fire energy, this love, this desire for the Other is a gift and is our breath and sun. The writer enters into this kind of death over and over. The reality of all darkness, in creation, in humans, and in the cosmos is where the fire and air is born. "Our stupid self-consciousness, our insufferable egos," as Keillor reminds us, wait for cleansing. Beneath the writer's hand, the earth already glows.

---

[44]Berry, 90, 91.

# 4
# Text: Marking the Stone

One of the functions of art is to awaken. We are overstimulated people with glazed eyes, missing the marvelous which passes before us and then is gone. We have domesticated life and truth and reduced it with our speech. We need artistic writing.

Before I came to do the lectures with which this book originated, my grandchildren offered me some jokes to awaken my audience. Among the "pearly gates" group was the story about the taxi driver who was given a lovely mansion in heaven, while the preacher got a modest cottage. St. Peter's reason was that people slept through the sermons, but prayed in the taxis. I would like to take you on a New York taxi ride for this last chapter, zipping along with inches between vehicles, and daring to pass without visibility. And keep you praying. By the time the fourth chapter comes along, those of you who have stayed with me will hope for the final revelation.

This final chapter, however, like a poem, will not be the final word. The elements may be elemental, but the work they do is ever mysterious and in various levels of chemical relationship. Creative writing is an attempt to find the elemental, but is it possible to find it, the essence in this postmodern world? Poet Charles Wright writes that essence must include everything. And still we seek, reaching for definition. Surely essence includes discovery and recovery of what has been lost. It is the thrill of correction, unsettling what once seemed to be truth, and offering new light. It is Jacob wrestling for the blessing.

I chose "Text: Marking the Stone" as a title because I am convinced that the challenge to leave markings about our place in time is to be faithful to the work. The Bible includes the instruction to "write it down," and the quotations of what has been written are frequent. "As it is written," Jesus said more than once. He trusted the text.

The earliest markings of ancient civilizations were held in reverence; the very act of symbols for speech held special powers. In some cultures the papyrus was soaked in water so that the inked words could be drunk, and thus give knowledge. Today we recycle words by the ton every day. How possibly could one book of stories or essays or poems be significant enough to mark the stone? And who should do it? What matters enough to write it down? What will stay?

John Haines, an American poet, writes about "the hole in the bucket" in contemporary American poetry. Poetry finally outgrew the academy in the 60s and became more accessible, but too often lacks ideas and vision.[45] The trend has moved toward recording personal experience as enough in itself, anecdotes which do not lead to an epiphany. "Does this poem grow out of necessity?" my teacher Peter Everwine would ask in our workshop. Did the writer merely contrive to make something—art for art's sake? And was it only broken-up prose?

Walter Brueggemann says that truth greatly reduced in our world requires us to be poets who speak against a prose world. By prose he means a world that is organized in settled formulae, "so that even pastoral prayers and love letters sound like memos. . . . By poetry I mean language that moves like Bob Gibson's fast ball, that jumps at the right moment, that breaks open old worlds with surprise, abrasion, and pace." He wants poetry, not moral instruction or problem solving or doctrinal clarification. He calls for "the ready, steady, surprising proposal that the real world in which God invites us to live is not the one made available by the rulers of this age."[46] I believe that his call, directed to preachers, applies to the faithful writer. The poet is invited to be a prophet, speaking in a voice that "shatters settled reality and evokes new possibility in the listening assembly." We are invited to destabilize the settled facts and open the way for transformation and something new.[47]

Mary Oliver in her book of essays *Blue Pastures* writes that the creative person is out of love with time and pushes toward eternity. She discourages the childish centering of poems "about me" to a movement that is anchored in valorous responsibility to the work. This means a willingness to enter the wilderness

---

[45]Donald Hall, ed., *Claims for Poetry* (Ann Arbor: University of Michigan Press, 1982), 131.

[46]Walter Brueggemann, *Finally Comes the Poet* (Minneapolis: Fortress Press, 1989), 3.

[47]Brueggemann, 4-5.

where ideas come in restless and disorderly ways, where the edge is its concern. She writes, "I have wrestled with the Angel and am stained with light," and she calls to the writer "to be loyal to the inner vision whenever and however it may arrive."[48]

My fellow Mennonite poets are fine examples of courageous writing in this numbed world. Julia Kasdorf with her poems and essays invites us to challenge the norms, and thus to help shape "the body," the community of faith, with our writing. Only writers who transgress are taken seriously, she writes.[49] Jeff Gundy in his recent paper at the Goshen writers conference, challenged us to act in the tradition of our heritage by being oppositional, even heretical.[50] These poets and others writing out of Mennonite heritage have often chosen to be at the edge of community, or out of it, to maintain an unencumbered vision. The argument will not be settled, whether the artist is most effective within or without. But some of us find ourselves in both places, and traveling.

In my most recent collection of poems, *Piano in the Vineyard*, I continue on my journey toward vision. I believe that poetry is a text which can render a world in which a reader may live with a fresh sense of what is home. Life can be disclosed and opened, some certitudes can be broken so that we can redecide. We can lift our imaginations to test our ideologies so that a new word, a new risk and possibility might open to us. We can challenge the culture.[51]

In the last poem of *Tasting the Dust*, I say that the mountain breaks down for us, creating our fertile valley, this mountain which rose in fire, and now offers its broken rock, vegetation, and water for our nourishment. That poem and others in the last collection seemed to be leading me to write about the world's brokenness, to bear witness to it, and to be involved in

---

[48]Mary Oliver, *Blue Pastures* (New York: Harcourt Brace, 1995), 4-7.

[49]Julia Kasdorf, *The Body and the Book* (Baltimore: Johns Hopkins University Press, 2001), 95, 182.

[50]Jeff Gundy, "Heresy and Individual Talent," paper presented at the "Mennonite/s Writing" conference, Goshen, Indiana, October 2002. Also available online in the December 2002 issue of *Mennonite Life* at <http://www.bethelks.edu/mennonitelife/2002dec/gundy_essay.php>

[51]Brueggemann, 10.

it. In the new book in the opening poem entitled "Egrets," I observe a flock of egrets flying in and out of the pine trees and clustering around a muddy pool. They surprise me because for years I have seen only one at a time—"simple in her full/ attention like/ a lily." Their agitation and the "brown muck splashing/ against their white/ breasts" shatters my image of them as elegant, clean and solitary. "They bend now/ toward earth/ and each other,/ up to their knees/ in commotion."[52]

Separation from the world. Engagement in the world. Duane Friesen makes a strong call for the artist, citizen, and philosopher to honor connections and intersections. "We do not have to choose between 'being' the church and 'connecting' with the larger culture. Rather, we must do both."[53] Gregory Wolfe, editor of *Image* magazine, a journal of religion and the arts, writes about the evangelical legacy of cultural separatism, of treating only some authors and publishers as officially approved and therefore safe. (The fiction writer James Calvin Schaap reminds us that the safe bookstores continue, however, to sell the Bible with all its scandalous stories.) But that separation is changing. Wolfe writes, "There are signs that many evangelicals are abandoning a brittle and triumphalistic stance, and searching for a vision that encompasses mystery, ambiguity, sacramentalism, and even tragedy."[54] That change allows the artist, the writer, to be a voice in that culture. I have said earlier that the faithful writer cannot remain elevated and clean above and beside the flow of the creek. The writer has mud on his white feathers, and a wail in his belly.

In the first section in *Piano in the Vineyard* I gather poems of lament for sorrows and brokenness. In the poem "In January" I lament those who die because of guns.[55] I recall the weeping of Joseph when he recognizes his brothers, and the centuries of hatred unresolved, the tragedy of Hiroshima, the cancers which

---

[52]*Piano in the Vineyard*, 4.
[53]Friesen, 25.
[54]Gregory Wolfe, "The Christian Writer in a Fragmented Culture," *IMAGE: a Journal of the Arts and Religion* 7 (fall 1994): 96.
[55]*Piano in the Vineyard*, 6.

"Move mountains higher than our faith."[56] I close this section with "Broken Places" in which I recall the comfort of a hot springs rising out of the mountain where its "heart/ spills out, holding us in its own/ broken place, the mists rising."[57]

The writer is asked to enter the pain of his or her own life, and the world, to be willing to reach into the fire, while the reader stands behind the tree watching. This is where the possibility of transformation arises, when we write from our own deepest fires. Using a different metaphor, Frederick Buechner writes that he thinks of painting and music as subcutaneous arts. They get under your skin. Writing on the other hand strikes him as intravenous. The words go directly into the bloodstream and go into it at full strength. He quotes Red Smith who said, "Writing is really quite simple; all you have to do is sit down at your typewriter and open a vein." And Buechner agrees. The only books worth reading are books written in blood. Write about what truly matters to you, not just things to catch the eye of the world, but things to touch the quick of the world the way they have touched you to the quick. We need wit and eloquence, style and relevance, but at the center we need the passion.[58]

Poetry is a response to the three basic questions: where do we come from, where are we going, and how do we live in the meantime? For writers of the Christian faith, the answers are given in the Text, the Scriptures, and always reinterpreted by words and lives. Scott Cairns is a poet among others who confirms the sacramental naming of the world, believing that it is suffused with meaning. Anabaptists both confirm the world and disconfirm. Jeff Gundy affirms the necessary marginality for poets, to be in culture and not of it. And from James Juhnke these words: we have the Gospel; take it and revise the world. These various voices are really one: the faithful writer participates in the ongoing creativity of God in this world.

---

[56]*Piano in the Vineyard*, 15.

[57]*Piano in the Vineyard*, 20.

[58]Frederick Buechner, *Listening to Your Life* (San Francisco: HarperSanFranciso, 1992), 190.

What are some of the characterizations of this participation? As I said earlier, the writer is called into the wilderness, into the unknown and unfamiliar.

*Wilderness*

In all of us, the wilderness,
our nostrils flared for water,
for the crouching shadow.

We glimpse it in dreams
and in the faces of children,
their eyes glancing into

another place. In adolescents
the tender profile—Pietro's
"Young John the Baptist,"

the golden curls, and under the smooth
cheek, muscles twitching.
Sometimes on a summer evening

the air presses against
our bodies with a stillness
so thin, we could break through.

Coyote call, the hawk's scream,
all of us thirsty for the unknown
as the snowmelt diminishes

into an eerie silence.
To cross over into that country
without map or tools,

to touch the source,
to kneel down and taste it.[59]

---

[59] *Piano in the Vineyard*, 61.

Writers enter unknown territory when they allow the work itself to move them toward its own intention. Characters in novels will "decide" the next move, the final development. Images in a poem take a turn quite unexpected, leading to imagination and memory which was forgotten. Even the use of a word or phrase, its sound, its rhythm, determines the development of meaning, and discovery. This is participation in the creativity of God for the kingdom.

I was fascinated to discover that the small butler's pantry which is my study, was originally a room for raising canaries. I was sitting in a space once full of bird song, seeds, and bird-do! It required a response in poetry, I thought. So I began simply describing a canary in a cage, caught and far from his original home, the Canary Islands where the native flocks live. The poem moved to a particular opera, Verdi's "La Traviata," and its powerful melodies, partly because I had recently been listening to it. And the poem reached into the questions of tragedy. Not until I allowed myself to try to find language for those final, devastating chords, did I know what to say about them.

> Page after page,
>     the writhing twists,
>
> the search for resolution.
>     Listen to the cadences
>         that lead to death.
>
> Notice what is gained
>     in those last chords: Love,
>         older than the world, gazes at you.[60]

As the poet participates in the creativity of God in the world, he seeks for some order in the chaos. Frost's "momentary stay against confusion" is an admission that poetry does not offer answers, but in its questioning it may at least grant a glimpse of order. For the writer of Christian faith, the questions of where

---

[60]*Piano in the Vineyard*, p. 64.

we come from and where we are going are partially answered in our creeds or confessions of faith, but are always in need of enlarged vision and transformation. Frank Burch Brown says that the arts are never ancillary to faith. We require them because they create secondary worlds—of sound and space, line and color, of pattern and word and image—that confront us with realities both human and divine, which we would otherwise ignore or fail to discern. They have the power, in fact, to convert our flaccid and empty souls into vigorous new creations. In order thus to transform us, the arts need not be overtly religious in either form or content.[61]

The question of " how we live in the meantime" raises the conflicting opinions of poetry which is political or didactic. Also it questions the act of writing poetry in a time of evil and horror. Czeslaw Milosz struggled with his passion for poetry. He wrote, "Poetry, after all, is embedded in the humanistic tradition and is defenseless in the midst of an all-pervading savagery. The very act of writing a poem is an act of faith; yet if screams of the tortured are audible in the poet's room, is not his activity an offense to human suffering?" As he puts it in one of his poems in 1945 during the war, "What is poetry which does not save/nations or people?" For him, poetry became not so much a weapon as a witness against evil.[62]

Denise Levertov wrote this: "A poetry articulating the dreads and horrors of our time is necessary in order to make readers understand what is happening, really understand it, not just know *about* it but feel it: and should be accompanied by a willingness on the part of those who write it to take additional action towards stopping the great miseries which they record.... And a poetry of praise is equally necessary, that we not be overcome by despair but have the constant incentive of envisioned positive possibility—and because praise is an irresistible impulse of the soul. But again, that profound impulse—the radiant joy, the awe of gratitude—is trivialized if

---

[61]Frank Burch Brown, quoted by Ralph C. Wood, review of *Good Taste, Bad Taste, and Christian Taste*, by Frank Burch Brown, in *Image* 32 (fall 2001): 122.
[62]Nathan and Quinn, 24-27.

its manifestations do not in some way acknowledge their context of icy shadows. . . . A sense of moral obligation has never and can never be the *source* of art even though it may be one of its factors. It is a question of that *context* being palpable in the work although perhaps never named, never made explicit."[63] Levertov speaks of the Old Testament prophets as providing the example of witness for western culture.

In my new collection I bear witness to the losses and pain which are part of the predictable cycle of the garden. I enter once more some of the stories of my family who writhed in the hands of Stalin's world. I honor the faith of my parents in their life and death. When my father was a teacher in a one-room school in Saskatchewan, he was known as one who successfully taught four-part singing. In the poem "Learning to Sing in Parts" I imagine how "after the quarreling at recess" he taught his students "to listen, to hold a pitch/ and hum it, his head close/ to the small child." As they try two, three, or even four pitches at once, they learn "the world's secret... to enter/ and be close, yet separate."

To participate in the ongoing creativity of God means that we are part of the process of the Maker-Savior who carries the whole cosmos forward toward a final transformation.[64] William Dyrness writes that true making of art requires rigorous discipline and sacrifice, being called to a certain kind of death, and a joy of discovery when the artwork assumes a life of its own. We are then engaged not so much in self-expression as we are giving witness to the common grace inherent in the divinely created order—to a truth and power that want something new to be born.[65]

My most recent poems have been exploring some ecclesiastical and theological terms. I found myself writing about Glory, and wrote a poem about it in the form of a

---

[63]Denise Levertov, *New and Selected Essays* (New York: New Directions, 1992), 146-147.

[64]Jeremy Begbie, quoted by Ralph C. Wood, review of *Voicing Creation's Praise* by Jeremy Begbie, in *Image* 32 (fall 2001): 121.

[65]William Dyrness, quoted by Ralph C. Wood, review of *Visual Faith* by William A. Dyrness, in *Image* 32 ( fall 2001): 122.

catechism. I give definition to Glory as "the fire at the center of pain" with the purpose "to make us whole." Water washes the pain but "the fire cannot be put out… because it is Love." In Love, I say, the "fire and water are one."

The elements which appear in this poem probably came from preparing these chapters. I look back then at the poem "Reclaiming the Land," and its questions in light of this recent poem. I wrote about the separation of land and sea, God's order in creation, which seems to be still in chaos with threat from the sea. I asked about the upside-down tree, about true wind, true separation from the world, and about what is elemental in the Ruisdael painting, and what is hidden. Do my definitions of Glory, or Love, as both fire and water, in air and earth, present everywhere, offer one way to answer these questions, or to illuminate the questions? Glory is revealed in the roots of the tree, in both air and mud. Glory is in the wind when it prevents floods and when it pushes in the storm. Is it the hidden element which stirs in the canvas and in the color waiting to be found? Pain is present, evil is present, but Glory is in the process of overcoming and leading us to wholeness.

I have suggested that the elements themselves offer in their reality and in their symbolic richness a way to enlarge our understandings of the questions, and sometimes to even give partial answers. When we dare, as writers, to travel into new territories where truth can be newly born, we are being faithful.

In her small and mighty book *Holy the Firm*, Annie Dillard writes this: "What can any artist set on fire but his world? What can any people bring to the altar but all it has ever owned in the thin towns or over the desolate plains? What can an artist use but materials, such as they are? What can he light but the short string of his gut, and when that's burned out, any muck ready to hand? His face is flame like a seraph's, lighting the kingdom of God for the people to see; his life goes up in the works; his feet are waxen and salt. He is holy and he is firm, spanning all the long gap with the length of his love, in flawed imitation of Christ on the cross stretched both ways unbroken and thorned.

So must the work be also, in touch with, in touch with, in touch with; spanning the gap, from here to eternity, home."[66]

In the title poem, "Piano in the Vineyard," in which I explore this life of participation. Because I love the piano as a source of creative expression, I entered it in new ways for me with language about the experience of playing it, and hearing it played. And this led me to confirm the process of creation and recreation, of interpreting life experience.

I begin with pruned vineyards which remind me of cemeteries and the deaths of friends. I find solace in the piano, "my fingers pressing into the massive weight." As a new bride I find strength in entering "this giant wooden heart," practicing the repeated scales, the "shimmers of Ravel." I recognize that "the patterns and shifting chords" are not there for themselves but for the "vast stretches." Chopin enters as composer looking for "the harmonic shift and pace/ which will ignite the coal," so that at last "each blazes up whole in its beauty and sorrow." Rubenstein walks onstage, an old man, "stiff and small," yet he "plays a stream and then a torrent/ his hands like water." I conclude that the Vine of the vineyard models for us how to live and to die within the rhythms of the grape harvest. The striving ends, but the music continues. "Life and death as light as that,/ wheeling between earth and heaven, then spilling over."[67]

The faithful writer marks the stone with humility, with true witness, and with the breath of creation, the fire of God's love.

---

[66]Annie Dillard, *Holy the Firm* (New York: Harper & Row, 1977), 72.
[67]*Piano in the Vineyard*, p. 65.

# About Pandora Press

*Pandora Press is a small, independently owned press dedicated to making available modestly priced books that deal with Anabaptist, Mennonite, and Believers Church topics, both historical and theological. We welcome comments from our readers.*

*Visit our full-service online Bookstore:*
**www.pandorapress.com**

David Waltner-Towes, *The Complete Tante Tina: Mennonite Blues and Recipes* (Kitchener: Pandora Press, 2004) Softcover, 129 pp. ISBN 1-894710-52-5

John Howard Yoder, *Anabaptism and Reformation in Switzerland: An Historical and Theological Analysis of the Dialogues Between Anabaptists and Reformers* Anabaptist and Mennonite Studies Series (Kitchener: Pandora Press, 2004) Softcover, 509 pp., includes bibliography and indices. ISBN 1-894710-44-4 ISSN 1494-4081

Antje Jackelén, *The Dialogue Between Religion and Science: Challenges and Future Directions* (Kitchener: Pandora Press, 2004) Softcover, 143 pp., includes index. ISBN 1-894710-45-2

Ivan J. Kauffman, ed., *Just Policing: Mennonite-Catholic Theological Colloquium 2001-2002* The Bridgefolk Series (Kitchener: Pandora Press, 2004). Softcover, 127 pp., ISBN 1-894710-48-7.

Gerald W. Schlabach, ed., *On Baptism: Mennonite-Catholic Theological Colloquium 2001-2002* The Bridgefolk Series (Kitchener: Pandora Press, 2004). Softcover, 147 pp., ISBN 1-894710-47-9 ISSN 1711-9480.

Harvey L. Dyck, John R. Staples and John B. Toews, comp., trans. and ed. *Nestor Makhno and the Eichenfeld Massacre: A Civil War Tragedy in a Ukrainian Mennonite Village* (Kitchener: Pandora Press, 2004). Softcover, 115pp. ISBN 1-894710-46-0.

Jeffrey Wayne Taylor, *The Formation of the Primitive Baptist Movement* Studies in the Believers Church Tradition (Kitchener: Pandora Press, 2004). Softcover, 225 pp., includes bibliography and index. ISBN 1-894710-42-8 ISSN 1480-7432.

James C. Juhnke and Carol M. Hunter, *The Missing Peace: The Search for Nonviolent Alternatives in United States History* Second Expanded Edition (Kitchener: Pandora Press, 2004; co-published with Herald Press.) Softcover, 339 pp., includes index. ISBN 1-894710-46-3

Louise Hawkley and James C. Juhnke, eds., *Nonviolent America: History through the Eyes of Peace* Wedel Series 5 (North Newton: Bethel College, 2004, co-published with Pandora Press) Softcover, 269 pp., includes index. ISBN 1-889239-02-X

Karl Koop, *Anabaptist-Mennonite Confessions of Faith: the Development of a Tradition* (Kitchener: Pandora Press, 2004; co-published with Herald Press) Softcover, 178 pp., includes index. ISBN 1-894710-32-0

Lucille Marr, *The Transforming Power of a Century: Mennonite Central Committee and its Evolution in Ontario* (Kitchener: Pandora Press, 2003). Softcover, 390 pp., includes bibliography and index, ISBN 1-894710-41-x.

Erica Janzen, *Six Sugar Beets, Five Bitter Years* (Kitchener: Pandora Press, 2003). Softcover, 186 pp., ISBN 1-894710-37-1.

T. D. Regehr, *Faith Life and Witness in the Northwest, 1903–2003: Centenninal History of the Northwest Mennonite Conference* (Kitchener: Pandora Press, 2003). Softcover, 524 pp., includes index, ISBN 1-894710-39-8.

John A. Lapp and C. Arnold Snyder, gen.eds., *A Global Mennonite History. Volume One: Africa* (Kitchener: Pandora Press, 2003). Softcover, 320 pp., includes indexes, ISBN 1-894710-38-x.

George F. R. Ellis, *A Universe of Ethics Morality and Hope: Proceedings from the Second Annual Goshen Conference on Religion and Science* (Kitchener: Pandora Press, 2003; co-published with Herald Press.) Softcover, 148 pp. ISBN 1-894710-36-3

Donald Martin, *Old Order Mennonites of Ontario: Gelassenheit, Discipleship, Brotherhood* (Kitchener: Pandora Press, 2003; co-published with Herald Press.) Softcover, 381 pp., includes index. ISBN 1-894710-33-9

Mary A. Schiedel, *Pioneers in Ministry: Women Pastors in Ontario Mennonite Churches, 1973-2003* (Kitchener: Pandora Press, 2003) Softcover, 204 pp., ISBN 1-894710-35-5

Harry Loewen, ed., *Shepherds, Servants and Prophets* (Kitchener: Pandora Press, 2003; co-published with Herald Press) Softcover, 446 pp., ISBN 1-894710-35-5

Robert A. Riall, trans., Galen A. Peters, ed., *The Earliest Hymns of the Ausbund: Some Beautiful Christian Songs Composed and Sung in the Prison at Passau, Published 1564* (Kitchener: Pandora Press, 2003; co-published with Herald Press) Softcover, 468 pp., includes bibliography and index. ISBN 1-894710-34-7.

John A. Harder, *From Kleefeld With Love* (Kitchener: Pandora Press, 2003; co-published with Herald Press) Softcover, 198 pp. ISBN 1-894710-28-2

John F. Peters, *The Plain People: A Glimpse at Life Among the Old Order Mennonites of Ontario* (Kitchener: Pandora Press, 2003; co-published with Herald Press) Softcover, 54 pp. ISBN 1-894710-26-6

Robert S. Kreider, *My Early Years: An Autobiography* (Kitchener: Pandora Press, 2002; co-published with Herald Press) Softcover, 600 pp., index ISBN 1-894710-23-1

Helen Martens, *Hutterite Songs* (Kitchener: Pandora Press, 2002; co-published with Herald Press) Softcover, xxii, 328 pp. ISBN 1-894710-24-X

C. Arnold Snyder and Galen A. Peters, eds., *Reading the Anabaptist Bible: Reflections for Every Day of the Year* introduction by Arthur Paul Boers (Kitchener: Pandora Press, 2002; co-published with Herald Press.) Softcover, 415 pp. ISBN 1-894710-25-8

C. Arnold Snyder, ed., *Commoners and Community: Essays in Honour of Werner O. Packull* (Kitchener: Pandora Press, 2002; co-published with Herald Press.) Softcover, 324 pp. ISBN 1-894710-27-4

James O. Lehman, *Mennonite Tent Revivals: Howard Hammer and Myron Augsburger, 1952-1962* (Kitchener: Pandora Press, 2002; co-published with Herald Press) Softcover, xxiv, 318 pp. ISBN 1-894710-22-3

Lawrence Klippenstein and Jacob Dick, *Mennonite Alternative Service in Russia* (Kitchener: Pandora Press, 2002; co-published with Herald Press) Softcover, viii, 163 pp. ISBN 1-894710-21-5

Nancey Murphy, *Religion and Science* (Kitchener: Pandora Press, 2002; co-published with Herald Press) Softcover, 126 pp. ISBN 1-894710-20-7

*Biblical Concordance of the Swiss Brethren, 1540*. Trans. Gilbert Fast and Galen Peters; bib. intro. Joe Springer; ed. C. Arnold Snyder (Kitchener: Pandora Press, 2001; co-published with Herald Press) Softcover, lv, 227pp. ISBN 1-894710-16-9

Orland Gingerich, *The Amish of Canada* (Kitchener: Pandora Press, 2001; co-published with Herald Press.) Softcover, 244 pp., includes index. ISBN 1-894710-19-3

M. Darrol Bryant, *Religion in a New Key* (Kitchener: Pandora Press, 2001) Softcover, 136 pp., includes bib. refs. ISBN 1-894710- 18-5

Trans. Walter Klaassen, Frank Friesen, Werner O. Packull, ed. C. Arnold Snyder, *Sources of South German/Austrian Anabaptism* (Kitchener: Pandora Press, 2001; co-published with Herald Press.) Softcover, 430 pp. includes indexes. ISBN 1-894710-15-0

Pedro A. Sandín Fremaint y Pablo A. Jimémez, *Palabras Duras: Homilías* (Kitchener: Pandora Press, 2001). Softcover, 121 pp., ISBN 1-894710-17-7

Ruth Elizabeth Mooney, *Manual Para Crear Materiales de Educación Cristiana* (Kitchener: Pandora Press, 2001). Softcover, 206 pp., ISBN 1-894710-12-6

Esther and Malcolm Wenger, poetry by Ann Wenger, *Healing the Wounds* (Kitchener: Pandora Press, 2001; co-pub. with Herald Press). Softcover, 210 pp. ISBN 1-894710-09-6.

Otto H. Selles and Geraldine Selles-Ysselstein, *New Songs* (Kitchener: Pandora Press, 2001). Poetry and relief prints, 90pp. ISBN 1-894719-14-2

Pedro A. Sandín Fremaint, *Cuentos y Encuentros: Hacia una Educación Transformadora* (Kitchener: Pandora Press, 2001). Softcover 163 pp ISBN 1-894710-08-8.

A. James Reimer, *Mennonites and Classical Theology: Dogmatic Foundations for Christian Ethics* (Kitchener: Pandora Press, 2001; co-published with Herald Press) Softcover, 650pp. ISBN 0-9685543-7-7

Walter Klaassen, *Anabaptism: Neither Catholic nor Protestant*, 3rd ed (Kitchener: Pandora Press, 2001; co-pub. Herald Press) Softcover, 122pp. ISBN 1-894710-01-0

Dale Schrag & James Juhnke, eds., *Anabaptist Visions for the new Millennium: A search for identity* (Kitchener: Pandora Press, 2000; co-published with Herald Press) Softcover, 242 pp. ISBN 1-894710-00-2

Harry Loewen, ed., *Road to Freedom: Mennonites Escape the Land of Suffering* (Kitchener: Pandora Press, 2000; co-published with Herald Press) Hardcover, large format, 302pp. ISBN 0-9685543-5-0

Alan Kreider and Stuart Murray, eds., *Coming Home: Stories of Anabaptists in Britain and Ireland* (Kitchener: Pandora Press, 2000; co-published with Herald Press) Softcover, 220pp. ISBN 0-9685543-6-9

Edna Schroeder Thiessen and Angela Showalter, *A Life Displaced: A Mennonite Woman's Flight from War-Torn Poland* (Kitchener: Pandora Press, 2000; co-published with Herald Press) Softcover, xii, 218pp. ISBN 0-9685543-2-6

Stuart Murray, *Biblical Interpretation in the Anabaptist Tradition,* Studies in the Believers Tradition (Kitchener: Pandora Press, 2000; co-published with Herald Press) Softcover, 310pp. ISBN 0-9685543-3-4 ISSN 1480-7432.

Loren L. Johns, ed. *Apocalypticism and Millennialism,* Studies in the Believers Church Tradition (Kitchener: Pandora Press, 2000; co-published with Herald Press) Softcover, 419pp; Scripture and name indeces ISBN 0-9683462-9-4 ISSN 1480-7432

*Later Writings by Pilgram Marpeck and his Circle. Volume 1: The Exposé, A Dialogue and Marpeck's Response to Caspar Schwenckfeld.* Trans. Walter Klaassen, Werner Packull, and John Rempel (Kitchener: Pandora Press, 1999; co-published with Herald Press) Softcover, 157pp. ISBN 0-9683462-6-X

John Driver, *Radical Faith. An Alternative History of the Christian Church,* edited by Carrie Snyder. Kitchener: Pandora Press, 1999; co-published with Herald Press) Softcover, 334pp. ISBN 0-9683462-8-6

C. Arnold Snyder, *From Anabaptist Seed. The Historical Core of Anabaptist-Related Identity* (Kitchener: Pandora Press, 1999; co-published with Herald Press) Softcover, 53pp.; discussion questions. ISBN 0-9685543-0-X
Also available in Spanish translation: *De Semilla Anabautista,* from Pandora Press only.

John D. Thiesen, *Mennonite and Nazi? Attitudes Among Mennonite Colonists in Latin America, 1933-1945* (Kitchener: Pandora Press, 1999; co-published with Herald Press) Softcover, 330pp., 2 maps, 24 b/w illustrations, bibliography, index. ISBN 0-9683462-5-1

*Lifting the Veil,* a translation of *Aus meinem Leben: Erinnerungen von J.H. Janzen.* Ed. by Leonard Friesen; trans. by Walter Klaassen (Kitchener: Pandora Press, 1998; co-pub. with Herald Press). Softcover, 128pp.; 4pp. of illustrations. ISBN 0-9683462-1-9

Leonard Gross, *The Golden Years of the Hutterites,* rev. ed. (Kitchener: Pandora Press, 1998; co-pub. with Herald Press). Softcover, 280pp., index. ISBN 0-9683462-3-5

William H. Brackney, ed., *The Believers Church: A Voluntary Church,* Studies in the Believers Church Tradition (Kitchener: Pandora Press, 1998; co-published with Herald Press). Softcover, viii, 237pp., index. ISBN 0-9683462-0-0 ISSN 1480-7432.

*An Annotated Hutterite Bibliography,* compiled by Maria H. Krisztinkovich, ed. by Peter C. Erb (Kitchener: Pandora Press, 1998). (Ca. 2,700 entries) 312pp., cerlox bound, electronic, or both. ISBN (paper) 0-9698762-8-9/(disk) 0-9698762-9-7

Jacobus ten Doornkaat Koolman, *Dirk Philips. Friend and Colleague of Menno Simons*, trans. W. E. Keeney, ed. C. A. Snyder (Kitchener: Pandora Press, 1998; co-published with Herald Press). Softcover, xviii, 236pp., index. ISBN: 0-9698762-3-8

Sarah Dyck, ed./tr., *The Silence Echoes: Memoirs of Trauma & Tears* (Kitchener: Pandora Press, 1997; co-published with Herald Press). Softcover, xii, 236pp., 2 maps. ISBN: 0-9698762-7-0

Wes Harrison, *Andreas Ehrenpreis and Hutterite Faith and Practice* (Kitchener: Pandora Press, 1997; co-published with Herald Press). Softcover, xxiv, 274pp., 2 maps, index. ISBN 0-9698762-6-2

C. Arnold Snyder, *Anabaptist History and Theology: Revised Student Edition* (Kitchener: Pandora Press, 1997; co-pub. Herald Press). Softcover, xiv, 466pp., 7 maps, 28 illustrations, index, bibliography. ISBN 0-9698762-5-4

Nancey Murphy, *Reconciling Theology and Science: A Radical Reformation Perspective* (Kitchener, Ont.: Pandora Press, 1997; co-pub. Herald Press). Softcover, x, 103pp., index. ISBN 0-9698762-4-6

C. Arnold Snyder and Linda A. Huebert Hecht, eds, *Profiles of Anabaptist Women: Sixteenth Century Reforming Pioneers* (Waterloo, Ont.: Wilfrid Laurier University Press, 1996). Softcover, xxii, 442pp. ISBN: 0-88920-277-X

*The Limits of Perfection: A Conversation with J. Lawrence Burkholder* 2nd ed., with a new epilogue by J. Lawrence Burkholder, Rodney Sawatsky and Scott Holland, eds. (Kitchener: Pandora Press, 1996). Softcover, x, 154pp. ISBN 0-9698762-2-X

C. Arnold Snyder, *Anabaptist History and Theology: An Introduction* (Kitchener: Pandora Press, 1995). ISBN 0-9698762-0-3 Softcover, x, 434pp., 6 maps, 29 illustrations, index, bibliography.

## Pandora Press
33 Kent Avenue Kitchener, ON N2G 3R2

Tel.: (519) 578-2381 / Fax: (519) 578-1826
E-mail: info@pandorapress.com
Web site: www.pandorapress.com